The Seal Pup

JAMES OTIS THACH

ILLUSTRATED BY WARREN CUTLER

BOWRIDER PRESS

Text copyright © 2010 by James Otis Thach.
Illustrations copyright © 2010 by Warren Cutler.

All right reserved. No part of this book may be reproduced or utilized in any form or by any means, electronic or mechanical, including photocopying and recording, or by any information storage and retrieval system, without written permission from the Publisher.

Inquiries should me emailed to Permissions@BowriderPress.com.

Published by Bowrider Press, Los Angeles

ISBN-13: 9780982566305
ISBN-10: 0982566301

Printed and bound in China by Global PSD, www.globalpsd.com

Channel Photographics & Global Printing, Sourcing & Development (Global PSD), in association with American Forests and the Global ReLeaf programs, will plant two trees for each tree used in the manufacturing of this book. Global ReLeaf is an international campaign by American Forests, the nation's oldest nonprofit conservation organization and a world leader in planting trees for environmental restoration.

PUBLISHER'S CATALOGING-IN-PUBLICATION
(Provided by Quality Books, Inc.)

Thach, James Otis, 1969-
   The seal pup / by James Otis Thach ; illustrated by Warren Cutler. -- 1st ed.
     p. cm.
   SUMMARY: In this rhyming story, a seal pup, separated from his herd, must find his way from the Arctic Circle to the California coast. The pup encounters penguins, killer whales, sharks, polar bears, walruses, and other marine mammals.
   Audience: Ages 5-12.
   LCCN 2009911395
   ISBN-13: 9780982566305
   ISBN-10: 0982566301

   1. Seals (Animals)--Juvenile fiction. 2. Animal migration--Juvenile fiction. [1. Seals (Animals)--Fiction. 2. Animal migration--Fiction. 3. Stories in rhyme.] I. Cutler, Warren, ill. II. Title.

PZ8.3.T2355Sea 2010   [E]
                                QBI09-600231

To the seal pup who inspired this story, many be your days,
And to Tina and to Grover, who are in my thoughts always
-J.O.T.

For my wife and son who helped in many,
many ways to complete this project
-W.C.

Below the frozen Arctic rim, upon the Bering Sea,

An island rises from the waves, as barren as can be.

In winter, when the northern winds blow icy night and day,

It seems as if no living thing has ever passed this way.

But when the weather warms a bit and skies turn bright and clear,

A herd of seals swims from the south and makes its landing here.

As soon as they have settled in, the mothers bear their pups,

Then spend the summer nursing them and watching them grow up.

By fall the pups know almost all they'll ever need to know,

So when the wintry winds return, they join the herd and go.

They swim three thousand miles to a sunny southern shore,

And there they stay until the springtime calls them north once more.

One year, a tiny pup was born—he was his mother's first—
And from the moment he first barked, she felt her heart would burst.
She touched his nose and barked hello and licked his face and hide,
Then settled down, contented, as he suckled at her side.
Even when they slept, her flipper stroked him through the night,
So he would know that she was near and never wake in fright.
And in the day he played with her and nestled at her side,
But never dared to swim out deep or in the ebbing tide;
For he had seen the scars on hides that spoke of dreadful bites,
And he had heard the bull seals roar, and watched their awful fights.
And once he'd seen a seal swim past the reef and disappear,
And every time he thought of it, it filled his mind with fear.

Autumn came, and then it was his mother's turn to fret,
For soon they would be leaving, and he wasn't ready yet.
She took him to the tidal pools to teach him how to swim;
He struggled just behind her as she softly called to him.
One evening as the seal herd slept, the Arctic wind descended,
And even in their dreams the seals all knew their stay had ended.
At dawn a snowflake found its mark upon an old bull's nose,
Which woke him from his heavy sleep, and slowly he arose.

He watched the clouds and sniffed the wind and barked a loud decree
Then shuffled to the water's edge and slipped into the sea.
The other bull seals roused themselves and followed one by one,
And mothers nudged their pups, for the migration had begun.
The pup awoke to find the beach alive with the commotion,
As waves of eager seals stampeded toward the seething ocean.
His mother tried to push the frightened pup into the sea,
But every time he struggled back, protesting desperately.

She looked around the empty beach and panic filled her heart—
It wasn't wise for them to be the last ones to depart.
For when the herd heads out to sea they make a mighty din,
And all the bodies in the water bring the hunters in.
At last she grabbed him by the scruff and held him in her teeth
And carried him from shore, beyond the safety of the reef.
She raced to join the herd with all the strength that she could find,
But with the burden of the pup, she soon fell far behind.
And then she heard a flutter as two seagulls rose in flight
And where they'd been, a jagged fin flashed in and out of sight.
She turned back toward the island, but they'd never make it there,
And clinging to her pup, she felt a shudder of despair.
But then she spied a tiny islet, just above the waves,
And knew if she could make it there, her pup might still be saved.

Held against his mother's side, the pup could look behind,
And what he saw would be forever frozen in his mind:
Two coal black eyes were rolling back, behind a pointed nose
That lifted up, exposing giant teeth in ragged rows.
It came so fast it seemed to him that they were standing still,
And now the shark was grinning as it closed in for the kill.
Its jaws shot forth—his mother twisted sharply to the side—
So close the pup could feel its rugged skin upon his hide!
He saw the creature spin around and felt his mother lurch,
As he was pushed above the waves and settled on a perch.

The ocean swelled around the rock and spray shot in the air,
But when he turned around, he found his mother wasn't there.
The pup embraced the slippery rock, awaiting her return,
As wind whipped off the water and the sea began to churn.
The rising waves swept over him until he lost his hold
And slipped into the writhing water, weak from fear and cold.
The waves took turns—one tossed him up, another smacked him down—
As if they were an angry throng that longed to see him drown.
But Nature has a way sometimes of coming to our aid;
When all looks grim and hopes grow dim, her kindness is displayed.
So just as he was giving up, a wave came from below
That gently raised the fading pup and laid him on a floe.
Steady through the raging storm, the pup was carried forth—
But though it was a saving grace, the floe was heading north.

The noonday sun lit up the sky and shone down bright and warm
Upon the sleeping pup, who lay exhausted from the storm.
The floe had drifted far from land and out onto the seas,
Whose bluster from the night before had faded to a breeze.
Then from the tranquil water, something curious sprang up
And landed on the gleaming floe beside the sleeping pup.

A penguin stood there, shaking off and taking in the view,
And then observed the pup and took a backward step or two.
Bursting from the sea behind him, six more birds appeared,
Each one looking at the pup and leaping back in fear.
But soon the birds determined that he didn't pose a threat,
And started to debate what sort of aid the pup should get.
Heading for the Southern Sea, they had no time to waste—
They'd just escaped the Anchorage Zoo, and feared they would be chased.
At last the tiny creature woke and hoarsely barked a plea,
And all at once the penguins turned and dove back in the sea.
But when they reappeared, their beaks were full of tasty krill
And one by one they fed the pup until he'd had his fill.

And when he fell asleep again, the penguins stood and stared
For something in the stranger made them want to linger there.
As evening fell, they huddled round to keep him from the cold,
And in the growing darkness, watched the Milky Way unfold.
And from that moment any thoughts of leaving him had ended,
For he was like their own now, to be nurtured and defended.

At noon they reached a field of pack ice floating in a bay
And settled on an outer floe to while an hour away.
They listened to the pack ice groan with every heave and shift
As floes collided, making one descend, the other lift.
At last they'd had enough of this and gathered up to go,
But as they did, a giant shadow passed beneath the floe.
An eerie calm descended as the penguins looked around—

Each one wondered what it was, but no one made a sound.
And then from underneath the flow there came a thund'rous crashing
That split the ice and sent the creatures flying, falling, splashing!

A killer whale had rammed the floe and now was circling back,

And heading toward the startled pup—his target of attack.

Within that fateful moment, seven penguins thought as one

And showed the selfless spirit in which all great deeds are done.

They knew the orca chose the pup to have the largest meal,

And so they came together in the image of a seal.

They hastened toward the killer, though it filled their souls with dread,

And started slowly spiraling around its giant head!

The hunter turned to follow them, abandoning the pup,

Who hurried to the nearest floe and swiftly scrambled up.

Then in a flash the whale attacked—but when it tried to bite,

The penguins split in seven ways and disappeared from sight.

They headed for the pack ice with the speed of frightened mice,
Erupting from the water and careening over ice—
Except for one, who ran head-on into the icy ledge
And bounced back in the water as the killer reached the edge.
The orca surged behind the penguin, flying through the air,
But when its giant jaws snapped shut, the penguin wasn't there!
The straggler landed near the rest, who burst into applause,
Amazed to see their friend so neatly cheat the killer's jaws.
Never had the ice felt better underneath their feet,
And no one could remember when the air had smelled as sweet.
The pup barked out his thanks to them for bravely interceding;
The penguins bowed with modesty, for such had been their breeding.

After they had caught their breath and laughed away their fear,

The group agreed to cross the ice until the coast was clear.

A half an hour after they had started on their walk,

A strange sensation told the pup that they were being stalked.

The feeling spread among the birds, and one by one they froze

And strained to see a sign of danger somewhere on the floes.

But all around them all they saw was gleaming, rolling white

As soon as he was under way, the birds came to his side
To offer him encouragement until he'd found his stride.
They taught him how to skim the sea, for which he showed a flair,
Stroking underwater and exploding through the air.
And when they reached a second floe, he barely stopped to rest,
Embarking on the waves again, his penguin friends abreast.

And when they broke, each penguin knew precisely what to do.
At first they fanned out casually, as if to look about,
But then one sidled toward the pup and pecked him on the snout.
Another charged him brazenly and nipped him on the ear,
And as the penguin mob advanced, the pup withdrew in fear.
They drove him to the water's edge and filled him so with fright
That, overwhelmed at last, he dove and swam with all his might.

When morning came the penguins rose, and it was time to go,
But much to their dismay, the pup refused to leave the floe;
For when he looked into the sea, each glint of light betrayed
A silent shadow slipping through the water, long and gray.
The penguin leader shook his head and stared down at the ice,
Then called them all to huddle, so to gather their advice.
In urgent tones the birds discussed which options to pursue,

As fields of pack ice sparkled underneath the blinding light.
Yet when they started up again, they walked with greater haste,
For none of them could shake the feeling they were being chased.
The pup kept looking backward till he saw a spot of black
That seemed to float above the ice and follow in their track.
They watched it as it hovered and then rose into the air,
And so exposed the tiny nose—of a giant polar bear!

Rearing on two legs, it gave three terrifying roars,

Then dropped back down and started running toward them on all fours.

The penguins hit their bellies and propelled themselves like sleds;

The pup began to gallop toward the ocean far ahead.

And oh, the ice felt cold and heartless underneath their feet—

The sea breeze blew against them as they made their mad retreat!

It soon became apparent that they'd never reach the sea,

And so the pup looked all about for other ways to flee.

And then he saw a burst of spray and heard two floes collide

And hurried toward the opening, the penguins at his side.

But just as they prepared to dive, the tiny window shut,
And each one felt an awful sinking deep inside his gut.
They huddled close together, for they'd nowhere to retreat,
And nothing left to wonder but how much the bear could eat.
And now it padded forward with its eyes upon the pup,
But as it did, it tipped the floe, and their side lifted up;
And quickly through the passageway the pup and penguins dove
And swam as far and fast as they could make their flippers go.

Underneath the heavy ice, the world was calm and bright,
A blue cathedral shimmering with gentle shafts of light.
And all their panic slipped away, their spirits made serene
As they beheld the wonders of a world they'd never seen.

That evening, as the sky lit up in shades of gold and rose,
They landed on a rocky beach to spend a night's repose.
The penguins soon were snoring, but their leader still was up
And hopped across the rounded rocks to sit beside the pup.
What a brilliant day they'd had, and what a lovely night!
There were no sunsets at the zoo—they just turned off the light.
The ceiling there looked like the sky, except it never moved;
The weather, although pleasant, never worsened or improved.
They'd never had to hunt for food or found themselves as prey,
But also never smelled the breeze or felt the ocean spray.
The penguin told the pup about their harrowing escape—
Sneaking past the sleeping guard and out the open gate.
Among the penguins, he alone was born into the wild,
Abducted by zoologists when he was just a child.
Though many years had passed since then, and memories were dim,
Within his dreams enthralling visions often came to him.
Sometimes he would see his homeland, stretching far and wide,
And on its gentle slope, a million penguins side by side.
It was to reach this distant land that he had hatched their scheme,
But privately he wondered if it wasn't just a dream.
He drew a breath and added, in a brighter frame of mind,
The journey was a worthwhile one, whatever they might find.

Then just as dark descended, they beheld a wondrous sight,
As colors crept into the sky and swept across the night!
The lights played on the water, and the water lit their eyes,
Till all the world was dancing with the fires in the sky.
They stared in silent wonderment, like peasants in a palace,
Enchanted by the autumn sky's aurora borealis.

A pale light spread across the east—the morning had just broken—

And by the barking of the pup, the penguins were awoken.

They yawned and blinked and stretched their wings and struggled to their feet,

Wondering what time it was and what there was to eat.

The pup was all impatience as he shuffled to the sea,

Diving while the others stood and watched him wearily.

Looks were passed from bird to bird, and each one shrugged and sighed,

Then waddled to the water's edge and dove into the tide.

Later, as the penguins fed, a salmon school passed by,

The sunlight on their silver scales enticing to the eye.

But when the pup swam after them, they spooked and sped away,

So shepherding the salmon school became a kind of play.

Swooping down from overhead, he made the school descend,

And then he'd creep from underneath, and up they'd go again!

And when he wished the school to turn, they silently obeyed,

Their flashing scales reflecting every motion that he made.

Then all at once they whipped around and caught him by surprise,

Dashing madly everywhere with terror in their eyes.

A hidden force was closing in and held the school in thrall,

Crowding them until the pup could hardly move at all.

He struggled to the surface where at last he saw the threat:

The school was being swallowed by a slowly rising net.

He heard the winch rope groaning as it pulled them through the air,

Then swung them, oh so gently, toward a vessel waiting there.

And on the deck, the hatches to the hold were open wide,

The gasping fish descending toward the blackness deep inside.

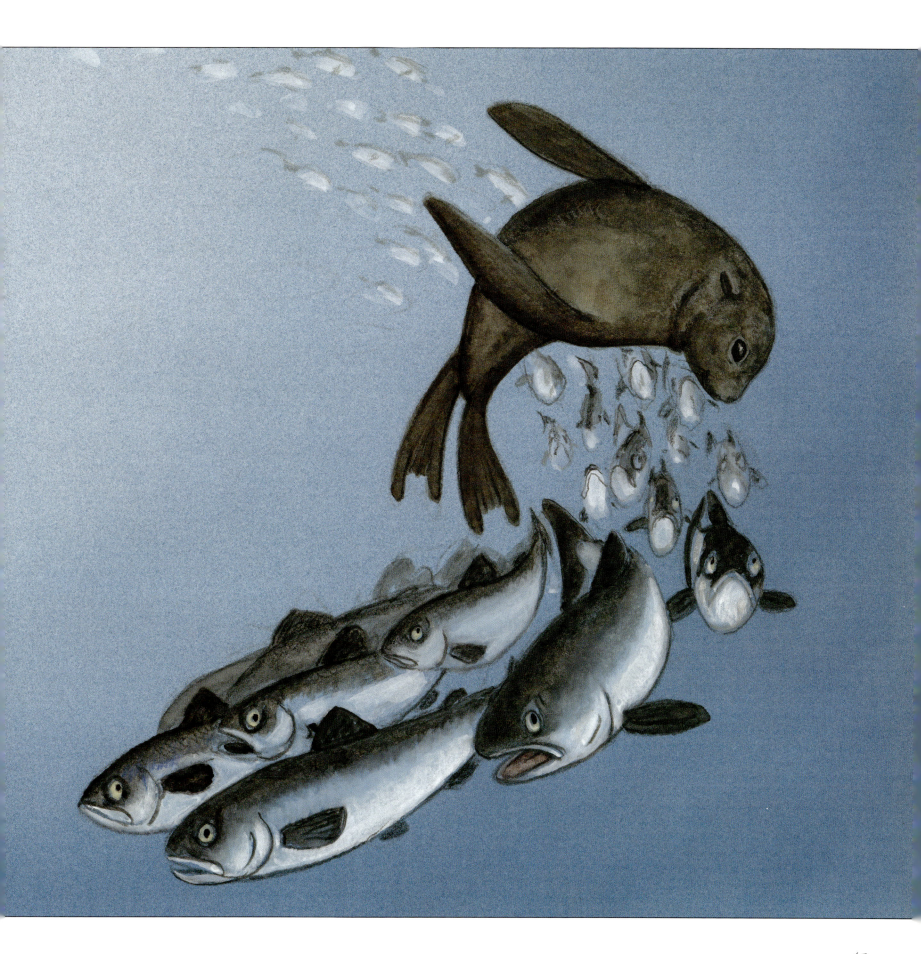

And how can one describe the night the pup spent in the hold—
The growing stillness of the fish, the darkness, and the cold?
It crept into his bones until his senses all went dull,
And he could barely hear the waves that lapped against the hull.

At dawn the hatch slid open and the net was slowly raised,

The pup ascending into sunlight, quivering and dazed.

The fish were dumped upon the deck and picked up by the men,

Who butchered them with flashing knives and dropped them down again.

And then, beneath the pile of fish, the seamen saw the pup

And shared a chuckle as their captain snatched the creature up.

He dropped it roughly on the deck and chased it up and down,

Jumping, shouting, stomping as it darted all around.

At last the captain cornered it—his men had laughed enough—

And reaching down a brutal hand, he grabbed it by the scruff.

He held it high for all to see, his fist around its neck,

And wound his arm as if about to slam it on the deck.

But then the creature bared its teeth—and sank them in his arm,

Which sent the captain flailing backward, wailing with alarm.

Suddenly the pup was soaring, falling toward the waves,
And heard the seamen roaring as their vessel steamed away.
His head was flushed with fever and his body stiff and weak,
And how he longed to close his eyes and drift away to sleep.
But all around, the only thing that met his searching eye
Was endless ocean underneath a cold, foreboding sky.
A tide of tears welled up inside that left his vision blurred
And nearly made him miss the flitting shadow of a bird.
A seagull circled overhead, and then came several more,
Their rising cries assuring him that he was close to shore.

High above the morning mist, a cliff rose tall and steep

Above a field of boulders where the pup could finally sleep.

But when he reached the water's edge and pulled onto the shore,

The boulder just before him spun around and gave a roar.

The pup had made his landing on a walrus colony,

And for this grave offense, was driven back into the sea.

He swam a few feet farther down and tried again to land,

But as before was greeted with a furious command.

One by one they shoved him off, and farther down he went

Until he reached the very end, his courage nearly spent.

And here an elder walrus sat, apart from all the rest,
Gigantic, with a broken tusk and scars upon his chest.
His eyes took in the tiny pup and then looked out to sea.
He murmured, "I suggest, young friend, you settle next to me."
The pup crept slowly from the waves, collapsing on the shore,
And all that day—and all that night—the walrus heard him snore.

His rumbling stomach finally brought his slumber to an end,
But looking round, he found that he was on his own again.
He shuffled to the water's edge and bobbed his head to dive
When suddenly the walrus surfaced, belting, "You're alive!
You slept so soundly, little friend, I half thought you'd expired,
But now that you're awake, I think some nourishment's required."
With that, the walrus vanished, but as quickly as he'd gone,
He reappeared—and in his mouth were mussels, clams, and prawns.
He laid them down before the pup and watched with much delight
His hungry guest ingesting every morsel in his sight.
The pup barked out a thank-you, but it turned into a yawn,
And soon he was asleep again, the walrus looking on.

At noon the pup awoke again and found a brilliant day.
He barked his thanks but added that he must be on his way.
"Of course you must," the walrus said, "and don't let me detain you.

I'm sure by now you've learned the secrets needed to sustain you."

The youngster waddled to the sea, then stopped and turned around,

His gaze returning to the walrus, knitted in a frown.

And from the corner of his eye the walrus saw his doubt

And hinted at the many skills no seal should be without.

"When tempests sweep across the sea and make the waters riot,

Where amid the chaos can you sleep in perfect quiet?

And when it's time to catch a meal, will you find better luck

Taking to the open seas or rooting in the muck?

If hunters come from underneath, then why is it absurd

To keep a watchful eye below, instead of watching birds?

Creatures who are slow to look are often quick to die,

But wisdom also comes from knowing when to close your eyes.

And if one day you're picked as prey, and sharks come after you,

Do you know the secret place where they cannot pursue?

But listen to me prattle on—you must be on your way,

I wouldn't dream of keeping you on such a splendid day."

Now the pup came back to him and barked a meek request.
The walrus sighed. "I s'pose I could, if you thought it was best.
Of course, there's only so much you could hope to learn from me,
But maybe I have learned a bit from forty years at sea.
Besides, my friend, just look at you—you're skinny as an otter!
We'll put some blubber on those bones before you take the water."
And so it was decided that the pup should stay a while,
And underneath the whiskers of the walrus was a smile.

Every morning, come first light, the pup would wake his friend,
To dive below the morning tide and glide around the bend.
They gathered piles of oysters from along the ocean floor—
The pup had never dreamed such feasts were buried near the shore.
The rooting stirred up clouds of mud, but with his eyes shut tight,
His sense of smell could find the shellfish quicker than his sight.
He learned to use his whiskers—and how useful they could be!—
For with them he could sense the slightest motion in the sea.

The walrus said, "No splashing—that's a foolish way to play;
The surface is where killers come when hunting for their prey.
Sharks are shrewdly colored—dark above and light below—
Which keeps them neatly hidden nearly everywhere they go.
Look at them from underneath—they blend in with the skies;
But from above, the darkness hides them right before your eyes.
They stalk you from the bottom and then rise to take a bite,
But as they near the surface, all the seabirds rise in flight.
No creature can out-swim a shark—they're much too strong and fast—
But if you pivot to the side, they'll likely swim right past.
And turn by turn you'll make your way across the ocean floor
Until, with luck, the shark gives up and you can reach the shore."

One evening when a storm blew up, they swam out to the deep
To find, amid the breaking waves, a quiet place to sleep.
"Don't ever ride a storm to shore, or you may well be crushed,
But if you slip beneath the waves, you'll find the ocean hushed."
With that, the twosome took a breath, and as they sank below,
The raging storm above them gently swayed them to and fro.
Now and then they drifted up to take breath of air,
Then sank again to slumber in the cradle waiting there.

On sunny days the walrus herd would gather side by side
To feel the warmth of fellowship and sun upon their hides.
And though the walrus longed to join his brothers by the sea,
The pup would not be welcome there, so it was not to be.
But one day while the pup lay sleeping, soaking in the sun,
The walrus watched his brothers and at last was overcome.
He shuffled very slowly so as not to wake his friend
Until he was beside the others, huddled end to end.
He heaved himself upon the pile and settled, nice and deep,
And bundled warm in walrus flesh, he drifted off to sleep.
The pup lay dreaming, weaving through the world that dreams impart,
When suddenly a passing cloud awoke him with a start.
He wondered where his friend had gone, and waited for a while,
Until he heard familiar snoring from the walrus pile.
He waddled over to the herd, gone ruddy in the sun—
A multitude in unity, with room for everyone.
And how it stirred his little heart, this world of warmth and kin;
What joy he felt to climb atop and nestle deep within!
And soon he lost himself in sleep and sank into a dream
As neighbors snuggled lovingly—or so at first it seemed.
One thrust up, to readjust his head against another
And saw the stranger lying there upon his sleeping brother.

His roaring seemed to shake the world, till all the herd arose
And ringed around the tiny pup, to rain a hundred blows.
The pup wheeled round in terror, but no matter where he turned,
Their tusks were raised in anger and their eyes upon him burned.
A brash young bull came forward, poised to crush the little pest,
But suddenly the elder walrus rose above the rest.
His voice rolled out like thunder's rumble from the cloudless sky,
And all stood still as statues underneath his flashing eyes.
"I may not be the youthful warrior that I used to be,
But I have fought a fight or two and tasted victory.
And whosoever lays a tusk upon my little friend
Will have to match his might with mine until the bitter end."
A silence fell as all eyes scanned around the shaking pup
To see if one was brave enough to take the challenge up.
And then the young bull dropped his gaze and settled to the ground,
And soon the others did the same, until they'd all lain down.

A path was left, just wide enough to let the two depart,

Returning to their usual place, together but apart.

Neither made a sound, for there was nothing they could say,

And sadness settled like a shroud upon the lovely day.

Late that night the pup awoke and dove into the sea

To pick a pile of oysters, clams, and sea anemone.

He laid them down beside the walrus, watching as he slept,

Then touched him softly with his nose, and turned around and left.

He swam all night beneath the moon, across the rolling deep,

And when he tired, he sank below the waves and went to sleep.

He dreamt of his adventures and the friends that he had known,

And with the dreams surrounding him, he didn't feel alone.

Setting out to sea alone was harrowing at first,

And any sign of danger always made him fear the worst.

A flapping wing would send him diving toward the ocean floor

To twist and turn in desperation till he reached the shore.

And only when on land, he'd see the sea still full of birds,

And realize an osprey's dive was all that he had heard.

But day by day the ocean seemed to open up to him,

Till he could scarce remember ever being scared to swim.

Once he saw a pair of mantas gliding side by side,
Their graceful wings in motion, as if flying through the tide.
They swam in perfect harmony, like dancers to a song,
Fading slowly into blue until the two were gone.
It left him with an aching that he couldn't understand,
As if some chamber in his heart was trying to expand.

One afternoon a storm blew in and made the sea go wild

But rocked the pup as gently as a mother would a child.

And then an eerie fog appeared and hovered, soft and pale,

As if to cover any sign that there had been a gale.

He swam along on the surface, for he couldn't quite resist

The slow unfolding mystery created by the mist.

Then through the haze emerged a bird with shiny yellow skin,

And blue eyes staring brightly in an optimistic grin.

The pup had grown quite lonesome on his own, week after week,

And so approached the bobbing bird and touched it on the beak.

The bird withdrew and turned away, its smile quite unchanged,

As if too haughty—or too dim—to join in the exchange.

Then appeared another with the same unblinking grin,

Its warm expression covering an emptiness within.

And then another, and another, every one the same,

Each one gazing far ahead and drifting without aim.

Suddenly the pup was spooked—he dove and swam away

And never saw the giant freight container gone astray.

Fallen from a cargo ship, it listed in the breeze,

Pouring forth a flood of rubber ducks upon the seas.

That night a sense of urgency arose within his mind—
A need to reunite with those he'd come so far to find.
And in a dream he saw them clearly, gathered on the coast,
And woke with the conviction that his herd was somewhere close.
The sun had not yet risen when he dove into the sea,
Bounding south with all his might, his spirits light with glee.
But soon he had to slow his pace as he became aware
Of something, sweet and sickly, hanging thickly in the air.
The odor grew, and then a puffin swooped from overhead,

Calling in a voice gone shrill with misery and dread.

"Black death! Black death!" she shrieked at him as round and round she whirled,

Then fluttered down the coast to scream her warning to the world.

The coastline curved into a bay, and there, within the sound,

A tanker tilted on the reef where it had run aground.

The pup could see a jagged gash that stretched along its side,

Pouring forth an endless stream of oil on the tide.

Already it had spread for miles, and would for many more,

Smothering the ocean waves and covering the shore.

It wasn't long before he saw the victims of the wreck,
Silent birds so blackened that they looked like silhouettes.
Others lay upon the surface, fallen to the scourge,
Their bodies floating listlessly, till slowly they submerged.
Fumes were rising from the oil and poisoning the air
Till all his senses filled the pup with sickness and despair.

He turned back toward the ocean but was halted by a sound—
A muffled bark that crossed the slick and made him whip around.
His eyes patrolled the distant shore until at last they reached
A spotted pup, beside her mother, lying on the beach.
Before them lay an open patch, where water met the sand;
The churning of the surf had kept the oil from the land.
To reach it, he would have to swim beneath this sea of death

Without a ray of light or any way to take a breath.
And if he lost his bearings as he made his way to shore
He'd be forever trapped between the oil and ocean floor.
But all his fears subsided underneath the rising urge
To reach that tiny window where their destinies converged.
He barked to her, to let her know that he was on his way,
Then took a breath and dove into the darkness of the bay.

The water underneath the oil was black as ebony—
A world so starved of sunshine, even shadows ceased to be.
And through the darkness giant globs of oil drifted down
With only their vibrations warning him to swim around.
And now his lungs were aching and he felt a pang of fear,
Uncertain of the way ahead or whether land was near.
Opening his eyes he saw a distant ray of light
And bursting with anticipation, swam with all his might.

He bounded, panting, from the surf and waddled onto land,
Careful to avoid the pools of oil on the sand.
He barked to greet the spotted pup and tried to shuffle near,
But she returned a growl so fierce, he backed away in fear.
She took her place beside her mother, lying on the sand,
Whose long and silent slumber she could still not understand.
And so the two remained apart, until the full moon rose,
And only then did he come near and touch her with his nose.
He sniffed the spots of oil that had settled on her fur,
And overcoming shyness, tried to lick the spots from her.
And when she fell asleep, he stayed beside her on the shore,
Stroking with his flipper as his mother had before.
The midnight tide crept slowly in and took her mother up
To carry her to sea again, and from her sleeping pup.

The two woke at the break of dawn to find themselves alone,
And saw with sudden horror how the oil slick had grown.
The pup was eager to depart and gave his friend a nudge;
She turned and faced the other way, too sick at heart to budge.
And when he barked impatiently, she settled on the sand,
Stating with her silence that she'd never leave the land.

The awful fears that gripped her, who but he could comprehend?
And so he shuffled near and took his place beside his friend.
Then all at once he turned and bit her smartly on the ear
And scampered toward the ocean as she galloped at his rear.
He darted underneath the waves and disappeared from sight,
And suddenly her loneliness was greater than her fright.

She dove to find him waiting for her on the ocean floor,
And held on with her flippers as he led her from the shore.
Moving slowly, through the shifting maze of oil they turned,
The pup employing all the subtle lessons he had learned.
And just as it began to seem they'd never reach leave the bay,
Up they surged, emerging in a burst of ocean spray.
What joy they felt to be again upon the open sea!
They dove and leapt—she crept behind and nipped him playfully,
He spun around and nipped her back, and so began a feud
Till neither knew which thrilled them more, to chase or be pursued.

They swam into the afternoon, then landed on an isle

To nestle in the silken sand and sun themselves awhile.

The pup dug up a feast of oysters just beyond the shore,

And with their hungers sated, they decided to explore.

They glided through a coral reef, a maze of pink and white,

Where brightly colored fish appeared, then vanished from their sight.

And then they slipped beyond the reef, along the ocean floor,

Seeking out what other jewels the ocean held in store.

Before them, through the haze and shadows, rose a ghostly form—

The wreckage of an ocean liner sunken in a storm.

What once had been the pride of men belonged now to the sea,

Its rigid bearing softened by an emerald filigree.

The ship appeared in perfect form, except along her bow,

Where just below the waterline, a rock had torn her prow.

The Spotted One was fascinated by the giant rip,

Moving quickly to it and then through, into the ship.

The pup held back, suspended by a tendril grip of fear,

For who could say what hidden danger might be lurking here?

But still, the Spotted One had gone, and couldn't go alone,

And so he swallowed back his fear and entered the unknown.

Inside it was as stately as a hundred years before,
Though creatures swam through portholes and crept sideways on the floor.
Behind the marble check-in desk, the mirror had turned green
But still held their reflections, which the pups had never seen.
And in the ballroom, chandeliers were swaying near the ceiling,
The gentle tinkling of their crystals endlessly appealing.
The carpets in the corridors were green with mossy bloom
And led the pups past empty cabins toward the engine room.

Here the carpet disappeared—the door stood open wide,
Beyond it utter darkness, hiding everything inside.
The Spotted One swam to it as if offering a dare,
The pup now sorely wishing they would head back up for air.
She turned in circles round the entrance, winking at his fear,
As something from the darkness slowly started to appear:
A crimson-colored serpent—with no eyes to guide its way,
Armed with rows of hungry mouths—came groping for its prey.
It coiled around the Spotted One, encircling her throat,
And in an instant placed a hundred suckers on her coat.
She writhed against it, bubbles bursting in a muffled yelp,
And yet the pup hung motionless, too horror-struck to help.
He felt like he was held again against his mother's side,
Watching as the jaws of death came toward him, open wide.
A second arm crept toward his friend, but as it neared her snout
She lunged and grabbed it in her teeth and madly shook about.
It wriggled and retreated, but the Spotted One held fast
Until the first arm loosened and she struggled free at last.
She bolted from the engine room, colliding with the pup,
Delivering the sudden jolt that finally woke him up.
He raced behind her, through the ship and out the giant tear
Back up to the surface where they filled their lungs with air.

The Spotted One moved slowly as they made their way to shore,
The pup a bit behind her, not beside her like before.
And when she finally fell asleep, the pup lay by her side,
But now the space between them felt a thousand miles wide.
His eyes were fixed upon the rippled path the moon had laid,
But in his mind the horrors of the engine room replayed.
And how the memory haunted him, until he fell asleep
And dreamt about the giant shark, still prowling in the deep.
It turned to him and as it grinned, he woke up with a start
And felt as if its rugged skin had brushed against his heart.

The Spotted One arose at dawn, her muscles stiff and sore,
And found the pup had laid a mound of oysters on the shore.
She ate the meal in silence, then they headed on their way,
But neither raced ahead or chased the other one in play.
They swam beside each other, never vying for the lead,
A shared awareness choosing their direction and their speed.

And then they came around a bend, and there ahead it lay—
Their herd, assembled in the harbor of their winter stay.
The elders slept on sunlit rocks, the youngsters swam and played,
And when they saw the Spotted One, what merriment they made!
They raced around her, up and down, surrounding her in bliss,
Now and then one dashing in to tap her with a kiss.
But no one saw the pup, who'd never played with them before,
Or noticed as he shyly turned and swam in toward the shore.
He found an empty patch of sand and waddled from the surf,
When suddenly a bull seal charged—for barging on his turf.
The pup jumped nearly from his skin, retreating with a yelp,
As up the beach a female rose to heed the call for help.
She barked and then was silent as she waited for reply,
Hoping that the one she'd heard would come before her eyes.
And then she saw him, running wildly, jumping rock to rock,
Leaping over sleeping seals awoken with a shock.
The pup was too excited to be mindful of the others,
Racing toward the primal sound that bound him to his mother.
And then they were together, and she licked behind his ears,
Her rapture overflowing in a steady stream of tears.
The pup could see a jagged scar that ran across her back,
A harrowing reminder of the terrible attack.

At last they settled side by side, and soon she fell asleep,
As he looked to the Spotted One, still playing in the deep.
And then his gaze went rigid and his hair stood stiff with fright,
For just beyond the splashing pups, two pelicans took flight.

He called out to the Spotted One, who turned to hear his bark,

The sea beside her thrashing with the gnashing of a shark.

Now its jagged fin rose up and cut across the bay,

Sweeping in a giant arc to isolate its prey.

Seals were bursting from the water, clamoring to shore,

Colliding with the others who had landed just before.

Still three pups were in the sea, beyond the others' reach,

Helpless as the hunter drove them farther from the beach.

A lonely rock protruded from the middle of the bay,

Just barely large enough to give two pups a place to stay.

But all three pups converged on it and tried to climb atop,

And every time one struggled on, another one would drop.

The shark patrolled in lazy circles underneath the seals,

Just waiting for the next to fall and make an easy meal.

The bulls were barking from the shore, but in their hearts they knew

The little ones were doomed, for there was nothing they could do.

The pup went to the water's edge, unnoticed in the din,
And with his eyes upon the shark, he silently dove in.
The moment he was in the waves, the roaring disappeared—
The pounding of his heart the only sound that he could hear.
He glided through the silted sea, his whiskers picking up
The movement of the hunter underneath the other pups.
And then he saw its mighty tailfin, sweeping side to side
Behind its massive torso, moving slowly through the tide.
He crept along beside its fins, so effortless and sly,
The hunter didn't notice till the two were eye to eye.

And still the shark kept circling, as if it paid no mind

To any creature crazed enough to sneak up from behind.

But deep within its lifeless eyes, a fury was concealed,

Just waiting for the moment to attack the little seal.

And then, in an astounding move, the pup began to thread

In graceful spirals, turning circles round and round its head!

Now the hunter shifted course, a little to the right,

To see if it could bring the creature close enough to bite.

The pup reflected every move, each subtle shift and sway,

Ushering the killer ever farther from the bay.

At last the shark could wait no more—its jaws came open wide,
Lunging with terrific force to plunge into his hide.
The pup had felt the tension rising just before the bite,
And sticking out his flipper, darted sharply to the right.
And now the chase was truly on, the pup just in the lead,
The killer bearing down on him with unrelenting speed.
The pup dove deep to twist and turn across the ocean floor,
But after each escape the shark was closer than before.
Down they went as silt and shadow swallowed all in gloom
Till from the murky ocean depths, the sunken vessel loomed.
It rose up like a demon from a dark and fevered dream,
Its gaping hole foreboding, as if frozen in a scream.
The pup went numb with terror but he sprinted for it still,
The hunter closing fast behind, a heartbeat from the kill.
The pup shot through the ragged hole and back into the ship,
The shark now slowing down before it followed through the rip.

The pup began a frantic search for someplace he could hide—
A darkened nook or cubbyhole to tuck himself inside—
Then slipped behind the check-in desk and settled to the floor,
Pressed against the boxes where the mail was kept before.
And then he saw the hunter coming, moving at a crawl,
Its green reflection stretched across the mirror on the wall.
And just when it appeared the shark would finally pass him by,
Something frightful from the darkness slammed into his side.

A moray eel had hidden in a mailbox by the floor

And lashed with savage anger at the stranger in its door.

The pup flew backward, into view, then swiftly shot away,

The shark exploding after, like a raptor for its prey—

Out the ballroom, down a hallway, round a colonnade,

Advancing ever closer with each motion that it made.

Past a blur of cabins, down a corridor they zoomed,

Until their path dead-ended at the dreaded engine room.

At last the race was over and the pup hung by the door,

The hunter coming slowly, knowing well what lay in store.

Its teeth came forth like daggers and its eyes rolled over white,

When suddenly the pup slipped back and disappeared from sight.

And now the hunter hesitated, harboring a doubt,

But even if it wanted to, it couldn't turn about.

And after all, there was this tender morsel to consume,

And so its grin returned as it went in the engine room.

The pup was huddled in a corner, hidden in the dark,

As dim light from the doorway cast the shadow of the shark.

And then he felt the phantom creature creeping from the back,

Its tendril arms unfurling through the swirling sea of black.

Keeping low, the pup moved slowly just above the floor,

Gliding underneath the shark and out the open door.

And then the stillness of the ship exploded in a boom,
As foe met foe, exchanging blows within the engine room.
The battle thundered through the hull, each mighty strike resounding
As creatures whirled like frightened birds with each percussive pounding.
The pup slipped through the frenzied ship and out the giant tear,
Then cast a final backward glance, and headed up for air.

Back along the cape, the herd sat huddled in their fear,
Staring at the waves, afraid the shark would reappear.
His mother's eyes moved blankly through the others on the land,
Then down to the impression he had left upon the sand.
Alone atop the tiny rock, the Spotted One still waited
And with each shimmer of the sea was fleetingly elated.
Only she among the herd had not yet given up,
A single light in all the world still burning for the pup.
The sun sank slowly from the sky and set the sea ablaze
Till finally the Spotted One was forced to drop her gaze.
But just as she was turning round to swim back into shore,
A barking came across the sea that made her spirits soar.
Then it came a second time, much closer now and clearer,
And then a splash of golden water, near and coming nearer.

And suddenly he sat beside her, panting on the rock,

The world around them silent as if time itself had stopped.

He tried to catch his breath, the water dripping from his fur,

Then turned to meet her gaze and gently touched his nose to her.

She nudged him back, and there they sat, against the close of day,

And watched the sunlight dance across the water in the bay.

And barking started in the herd that built into a roar,

For never had they seen so kind and brave a soul before.

A few months on, a crystal dawn lit up the Southern Sea
When from the water sprang a penguin, landing awkwardly.
He looked across an open field and then turned side to side
As six more birds appeared behind him, shaking off the tide.
The seven stared in silent wonder, taking in the view:
A million penguins staring back—one penguin's dream come true.

Acknowledgements

There are many people to thank for helping bring this book into being. The first and foremost is my brother and partner, Will, without whom none of this would be happening. Thanks, Will. To Warren, for saying yes to this project, for his endless dedication to it, and for bringing the story to life more beautifully than I could have imagined. To my local librarians at the West Hollywood branch, for giving me all the research materials I needed, and a quiet, cool place to read and write. To Alex Zorensky, my trusted research assistant and friend. To Joy Neaves, my first audience, who gave me early and important encouragement. To Sarah, for being a wonderful sister, and Dizy, for being a wonderful sister-in-law, and for introducing me to Joy. To Megan and Anna Campion, the first mother & daughter to read it, whose enjoyment of it gave me the sweetest taste of what it means to be an author. And to Megan alone, for being a lifelong friend, and for ongoing support and advice and editing talents. To Sapphira Fein, who was the first teacher to read it to her class, and who has been a joy to know ever since. To Dr. Carlo Honrado, for your kind heart and incredible talent, and for giving me back my smile. To April Halprin Wayland, for reawakening me to what children's books can do, and for believing in me. To Mrs. Spilker, my favorite teacher ever, who introduced me (in first and fifth grades) to the worlds inside books, and the world beyond them, and who was always clear-eyed and and always cared (and who now lets me call her Harriet). To Tina Pedone, for telling me to go for it, and for sharing the journey. To my grandmother Boo, for teaching me to rhyme, and to embrace life. To my parents, for everything. And to the real-life seal pup, whose brave and generous spirit inspired me, and to whom this story truly belongs. I hope you are well.

CREDITS

Editors:
Katya Rice
Alexandar Landfair
Chris Rager

Layout Artist:
Jacqueline Domin

Printer:
Global PSD

Website Design:
Scott Rodenhizer at NewPixel

Song:
Todd Spahr

Logo Design:
Amanda Brooks